BRIE

GOSPEL SPEECH

A fresh look at the
relationship between every
Christian and evangelism

LIONEL WINDSOR

matthiasmedia

SYDNEY · YOUNGSTOWN

Matthias Media
(St Matthias Press Ltd ACN 067 558 365)
Email: info@matthiasmedia.com.au
Internet: www.matthiasmedia.com.au
Please visit our website for current postal and telephone
contact information.

Matthias Media (USA)
Email: sales@matthiasmedia.com
Internet: www.matthiasmedia.com
Please visit our website for current postal and telephone
contact information.

ISBN 978 1 922206 81 7

Cover design and typesetting by affiniT Design.

CONTENTS

INTRODUCTION

We all have a different relationship with speech. Some of us love it, some of us... not so much. For some it depends a lot on the context: speaking on the phone with a friend is perfectly enjoyable; speaking publicly in front of an audience is our worst nightmare. Some of us speak at a million miles an hour, while others have a slow and measured pace, choosing every word carefully.

In many ways, speech really is an intrinsic reflection of who we are as individuals.[1]

It's not uncommon, for example, to hear it suggested that women speak considerably more words per day on average than men (20,000 vs 7,000 is the commonly cited statistic). Supposedly, talking

---

1   A point Jesus makes in Luke 6:45.

more is just part of a woman's nature. But this is not so, according to a study reported by *Scientific American*.[2] As it turns out, the average for men and women is basically the same.

Nonetheless, the same study did note that there was a big variation between participants. One man in the study averaged just 795 words a day, while at the top end of the scale another man averaged 47,000 words. I'm guessing those two guys had pretty different personalities, and it might be fun to play the game of guessing their respective professions: Monk vs auctioneer? Train driver vs telemarketer? Pastor on a Monday vs pastor on a Sunday?

It would be interesting to study a group of Christians, too, although not so much to study how many words they speak per day—I'm guessing it would be similar to the general population, notwithstanding the Bible's counsel for us to be "slow to speak" (Jas 1:19). Rather, it would be interesting to count how many *gospel words* they speak per day—words that tell of the gospel of the Lord Jesus and point others to his saving work on the cross and his life-giving resurrection.

---

2   See N Swaminathan, 'Gender jabber: Do women talk more than men?', *Scientific American*, 6 July 2007 (viewed 5 August 2015): http://scientificamerican.com/article/women-talk-more-than-men/.

For some Christians, perhaps even most of us, if such a study were done the number might be embarrassingly low.

For others of us, the number is low but there is little embarrassment. We've long since rationalized away any sense of guilt or failure: "I don't have the gift of being an evangelist"; "the Bible doesn't command me to speak of Jesus"; "I let my actions do the talking".

But if our speech really is an intrinsic part of who we are, and if being a Christian is a fundamental and even primary way we describe ourselves, then might we need to look again at what the Bible has to say about our speech patterns?

Perhaps it's time for a rethink and a fresh approach to the topic. Read on.

Ian Carmichael
Editor

1. ARE ALL CHRISTIANS COMMANDED TO EVANGELIZE?

Does God command every individual Christian to evangelize? Or is evangelism just a job for specially gifted individuals?

If you've been a Christian for a while, it's likely that these questions have popped into your head from time to time. You might remember an initial burst of enthusiasm for Jesus at some time in your life. Maybe you remember burning with a passionate desire to tell as many people as you could about the wonderful news of Jesus' death and resurrection. After all, this news had recently rocked your world and given you hope and life and meaning; why wouldn't you want others to know it? But by now, maybe, you're feeling a bit jaded. Of course, you acknowledge that the 'gospel', the message about Jesus, is quite important. But you've come to realize that you're not really the kind of person who feels comfortable talking about Jesus to other people. Maybe you just feel ill-equipped. Maybe it's not your personality type. Maybe evangelism just feels plain weird to you. Maybe you've had a few bad evangelistic experiences. Awkward moments. Maybe you've lost friends. Maybe you're getting fed up with that vaguely guilty feeling that nags away at you whenever preachers tell you to evangelize. And so you might be asking: does God really want me to do this evangelism thing anyway? Does he actually command it anywhere?

In fact, if you go hunting in the Bible for commands to evangelize, you won't find very much material. True, there's the 'great commission' in Matthew 28:19-20. Jesus, having just risen from the dead, says to his disciples, "Go therefore and make disciples of all nations", and then adds: "teaching them to observe all that I have commanded you". By applying the strict rules of logic, you can reason that "everything I have commanded you" includes the command to make disciples. So that means disciple-making is a command for all disciples, right?

Peter also tells Christians to "always" be "prepared to make a defense to anyone who asks you for a reason for the hope that is in you" (1 Pet 3:15). Paul tells the Colossians to use opportunities to speak to outsiders about "grace", which must have something to do with the gospel (Col 4:5-6, NIV; cf. Col 1:6).

But if you think about it further, these commands by themselves are a pretty flimsy basis for proving that God wants every individual Christian to evangelize. It's possible, isn't it, that "make disciples" is just a general command for the church as a whole. Clearly, the *church* is expected to evangelize. But that doesn't mean that I, personally, have to do it. Furthermore, the verses from Peter and Paul don't really prove much. Being ready to give an answer and to make the most of opportunities seems to assume that evangelism is a passive and sporadic activity at best. When was the last time anybody asked you to give an answer for the hope that was in you? Anyway, the 'evangelist' was a special role in the early church (Acts 21:8; Eph 4:11; 2 Tim 4:5). So some people suggest that these commands don't amount to very much.

But take a step back for a moment. Why are you looking for a command in the first place?

Normally we look for commands when we need a reason to do something unpleasant. When I tell my kids to eat their vegetables, they want me to give them a command with exact specifications. They ask: Do I have to eat all of the vegetables? If not, how many? Does that include the ones mushed into the potatoes? But it's a different story with chocolate. If I put chocolate in front of them, no command is required. That's because, for them, there's no reason not to eat chocolate. The same thing applies when we start asking whether we're commanded to evangelize. By asking the question we're treating evangelism like kids treat eating vegetables. We're saying that evangelism is technically a good thing to do, but we'd prefer not to do it unless we really have to. That should tell us that something has gone wrong somewhere.

In recent times, certain evangelists and writers have approached the issue in a better way. They've realized that it's not enough simply to scour the Bible for individual commands. Instead, they've asked a broader question: what patterns of mission did the Bible writers (e.g. Paul) expect to be happening in their churches? And how can we follow the same patterns?[3] This can be a more helpful approach, because it helps us to think in terms of bigger principles.

But in this book, I'm not going to follow that approach—because ultimately, it's not enough. There's something more fundamental; a truth that needs to grip us before we even start to think about commands or communities or church organization or pragmatics or patterns or gifts. We need to understand the relationship between human speech and the gospel itself. According to the Bible, there is something deeply and profoundly important about human speech, especially when we come to think

---

3 For a couple of practical books from my part of the world with different perspectives on the issue of individual evangelism, see *Know and Tell the Gospel* by John Chapman and *The Best Kept Secret of Christian Mission: Promoting the Gospel with More Than Our Lips* by John Dickson. For some more academic books about Paul's expectations for his churches, again with different perspectives, see *Mission-Commitment in Ancient Judaism and in the Pauline Communities: The shape, extent and background of early Christian mission* by John Dickson, *Paul and the Mission of the Church: Philippians in Ancient Jewish Context* by James P Ware, and *Paul's Understanding of the Church's Mission: Did the Apostle Paul Expect the Early Christian Communities to Evangelize?* by Robert L Plummer. This last book has been helpfully summarized by Kevin deYoung in his article 'Paul's understanding of the church's mission', *The Gospel Coalition*, 13 May 2011 (viewed 14 August 2015): http://thegospelcoalition.org/blogs/kevindeyoung/2011/05/13/pauls-understand-of-the-churchs-mission/.

about the gospel. In fact, the Bible often talks about human speech and salvation in the same breath.

You might have realized already that I don't like the title of my own chapter, 'Are all Christians commanded to evangelize?' I don't like the word 'commanded'. But actually, I don't like the word 'evangelize' either. It's too rubbery, and means different things to different people. What popped into your head when you read the word 'evangelize'? If I asked this question of ten different people, I'd probably get eleven different answers. From now on, I'm going to erase the word 'evangelism' from this book. Instead, I'm going to use the more useful, albeit more clunky, phrase 'gospel speech'. That will help us to get to the heart of the issue: What does the Bible say about how human beings use words to speak the gospel—to whomever, however, whenever?

Of course, that means we need to talk more about the gospel itself. And we will. In the rest of this book, we'll look at what the gospel has to say about various questions or objections to gospel speech:

- I'm not good enough.
- I'm not gifted enough.
- I'm not really a 'speaking' Christian.

1. ARE ALL CHRISTIANS COMMANDED TO EVANGELIZE?

- I can promote the gospel better by my good works.
- I'm not the mouth in Christ's body.
- I'm more comfortable speaking the gospel to insiders rather than outsiders.
- I can't do what they're doing.

2. SHUT YOUR MOUTH

"I'm not good enough!"

Maybe you think you're not qualified to speak the gospel to people because you're not godly enough. If you feel this way, then you're absolutely right and absolutely wrong at the same time. You're right that you're not godly enough. But you're wrong about the gospel.

Think about the great prophet Isaiah. When God revealed himself to Isaiah, it scared him out of his wits. Isaiah realized that he had a very serious speech problem:

> And [Isaiah] said: "Woe is me! For I am lost; for I am a man of unclean lips, and I dwell in the midst of a people of unclean lips; for my eyes have seen the King, the LORD of hosts!" (Isa 6:5)

This very same speech problem confronts us at the start of Paul's letter to the Romans. The book of Romans is a letter about the way God reveals himself to us. God reveals his gospel (1:1), his son (1:3-4), his power (1:16), his salvation (1:16), and his righteousness (1:17). But when God reveals himself, he also reveals something about *human* speech. And what we learn about human speech is not good. Whenever human speech is mentioned in the opening chapters of Romans (apart from Paul's own words), it's an unmitigated disaster.

In the very first chapter, Paul gives us a catalogue of general human miserableness and rebellion against God. Near the climax of this list, Paul describes us human beings as "gossips, slanderers, haters of God, insolent, haughty, boastful" (Rom 1:29-30). A short time later, Paul talks directly about our speech-organs—our mouths. Our mouths are diseased; they're intimately involved in our rebellion against God:

> For we have already charged that all, both Jews and Greeks, are under sin, as it is written:
>
> ...
>
> "Their throat is an open grave;
>> they use their tongues to deceive."

"The venom of asps is under their lips."
"Their mouth is full of curses and
bitterness." (Rom 3:9, 13-14)

Our mouths reveal what's in our hearts, and it's very bad. We know all too well the terrible power of our words; how our words can wound and break hearts and lives. This isn't a minor issue. The God who reveals himself is holy and powerful, and he is angry with our speech.

Romans also talks about another kind of revelation from God, a revelation that God gave to the nation of Israel many years before. This revelation is called the *law*. It's a very good revelation, because it shows us how holy and powerful God is, and it tells us what this holy God expects of his people. But the law-revelation provokes another serious speech problem. The people who have the law think that they should *preach* the law. They think that God gave the law to them so they could teach everybody in the world how to work hard and live better and please God:

> ...and if you are sure that you yourself are a guide to the blind; a light to those who are in darkness, an instructor of the foolish, a teacher of children, having in the law the embodiment of knowledge and truth... (Rom 2:19-20)

But preaching the law is crazy talk, because anyone who thinks he's qualified to preach God's law has the same problem as the people he's preaching to. Paul goes on:

> ...you then who teach others, do you not teach yourself? While you preach against stealing, do you steal? You who say that one must not commit adultery, do you commit adultery? You who abhor idols, do you rob temples? You who boast in the law dishonour God by breaking the law. (Rom 2:21-23)

In fact, law-preaching creates an even bigger speech problem. Whenever somebody preaches the law and doesn't keep it, they prove that God's word doesn't work. And that just makes the listeners scoff and slander God himself:

> For, as it is written, "The name of God is blasphemed among the Gentiles because of you". (Rom 2:24)

This all just goes to show that the law isn't there to be promoted or preached or proclaimed. In fact, the law isn't designed to make anybody talk at all. The law has the opposite purpose. The law is designed to *stop* us talking:

> Now we know that whatever the law says it speaks
> to those who are under the law, so that every
> mouth may be stopped, and the whole world may
> be held accountable to God. For by works of the
> law no human being will be justified in his sight,
> since through the law comes knowledge of sin.
> (Rom 3:19-20)

God's law-revelation is intended to bring silence.
And when I say 'silence', I'm not talking about quiet
religious contemplation. I'm talking about the silence
of a defendant in the dock who has been utterly
convicted by the weight of the charges against him,
and who simply has nothing to say. The law is there
to mortify us; to show us just how venomous and
bitter our sin really is. The law makes us accountable
to God. The law is there to render us speechless.
Only then will we hear the gospel.

And what is the gospel? It is not a list of God's
requirements for us to perform, but a message about
God's Son for us to hear and believe (Rom 1:1-5). It is
the message that we:

> ...are justified by his grace as a gift, through the
> redemption that is in Christ Jesus, whom God
> put forward as a propitiation by his blood, to be
> received by faith. (Rom 3:24-25)

Only in our speechlessness will we hear the gospel—the message of salvation, the death and resurrection of Jesus, which makes us right before our holy creator and judge (Rom 3:21ff). The law testifies to the gospel. But it's not the gospel.

So when God reveals himself, the first thing you need to do is to shut your mouth and listen.

In the next chapter, we'll think about another objection to gospel speech: "I'm not gifted enough".

3. GOD PUTS THE WORDS RIGHT IN YOUR MOUTH

"I'm not gifted enough!"

Maybe you think you're not qualified to speak the gospel to people because you're not gifted enough. But if you're a Christian, you already have the greatest gift in the world. It's a gift that makes you talk.

Throughout the Old Testament, we see a recurring pattern:

- sin
- salvation
- speech/singing.

This is how God works, according to the Bible. People sin against God, repeatedly and inexcusably. God is therefore rightly angry with people. But instead of simply judging them, he saves them, proving how powerful he really is. And then, once he's given them this great gift of salvation, God does something to their mouths. He puts a speech or a song in their mouths, and tells them to speak over and over again about how amazing his salvation really is.

Here are three places in particular where this pattern is clear: Deuteronomy 32, Isaiah 59 and Psalm 51. These are very significant parts of the Old Testament. In fact, the apostle Paul refers to them repeatedly in his letter to the Romans.[4]

Deuteronomy 32 is a song Moses taught to Israel just before they entered the promised land. It's a song they must keep in their mouths, singing it constantly, never forgetting it (cf. Deut 31:19, 21). It's a strange song for a nation to sing. In fact, it's the complete opposite of a national anthem. It's a song not about Israel's glory, but about Israel's shame. Israel, according to this song, is a rebellious nation. The Israelites deal corruptly with God. They aren't

---

4   Paul quotes these passages explicitly: Deuteronomy 32 is cited in Romans 10:19, 12:19 and 15:10; Isaiah 59 is cited in Romans 3:15-17 and 11:26-27; and Psalm 51 is cited in Romans 3:4. Psalm 32, another psalm about David being forgiven and then proclaiming God's word, is cited in Romans 4:7-8.

God's children. They are blemished and crooked and twisted and greedy and scoffers and demon-worshippers and perverse and cheats and foolish and venomous. Israel is powerless and weak and utterly corrupt. But God is powerful and righteous. He will show his power through Israel, both by judging his enemies and also by rescuing his powerless servants (e.g. 32:36). He gives Israel the great gift of salvation.

But even though the song is about Israel's sin and Israel's salvation, it's not just a song for Israel alone. It's a song that is put into Israel's mouth so that everybody else can hear how God helps those who can't help themselves. God doesn't just rescue his weak and foolish people; he also uses them as his global mouthpiece. Israel's job is to sing of God's greatness to the world:

> "Give ear, O heavens, and I will speak,
>> and let the earth hear the words of my mouth...
> For I will proclaim the name of the LORD;
>> ascribe greatness to our God!" (Deut 32:1, 3)

Isaiah 59 echoes this same pattern. The chapter describes the total depravity of Israel at a particularly dark time in their history. Israel's hearts, hands and mouths are defiled because they are not upholding

God's justice. Nobody, none at all, is doing what is right. But the uselessness of God's people doesn't mean that God himself is powerless. He is powerful; he will achieve his purposes to judge the world and to deliver Israel, despite their sin:

> He saw that there was no man,
> > and wondered that there was no-one to intercede;
> then his own arm brought him salvation,
> > and his righteousness upheld him. (Isa 59:16)

> "And a Redeemer will come to Zion,
> > to those in Jacob who turn from transgression",
> declares the Lord. (Isa 59:20)

What does God do once he's saved Israel? He gives them a role, a task. This task is to speak God's word—to have this word of salvation in their mouths and to declare the light of God's glorious power to the nations:

> "And as for me, this is my covenant with them", says the Lord: "My Spirit that is upon you, and my words that I have put in your mouth, shall not depart out of your mouth, or out of the mouth of your offspring, or out of the mouth of your children's offspring", says the Lord, "from this time forth and forevermore". (Isa 59:21)

And nations shall come to your light,
>   and kings to the brightness of your rising.
>   (Isa 60:3)

Psalm 51 is a song of David, King of Israel, written after he stole a man's wife and then arranged his murder. David is stricken, and begs for forgiveness. He realizes that he deserves nothing from God. But he knows that God's response to his sin will prove God's justice and power. In fact, his broken spirit and contrite heart will enable him to be a mouthpiece for God, to shout to the world of God's mercy and power:

Restore to me the joy of your salvation,
>   and uphold me with a willing spirit.
Then I will teach transgressors your ways,
>   and sinners will return to you.
Deliver me from bloodguiltiness, O God,
>   O God of my salvation,
>   and my tongue will sing aloud of your
>   righteousness.
O Lord, open my lips,
>   and my mouth will declare your praise.
>   (Ps 51:12-15).

For David, as for Israel, salvation affects the mouth as well as the heart.

Do you notice in all three passages that the singers are exactly the right people to sing the song? The song/speech is about God's salvation, not about human achievement. And so the singers/speakers aren't powerful people, or talented people, or upright people. They're weak people, broken people, sinful people. But when God saves these sinners, they also become gifted singers who sing (or speak) about God's salvation to the world. The gift they've received isn't a melodious voice, or a clever turn of phrase, or a quick wit. The gift is salvation itself. Since they've been saved from sin, they're qualified to talk about salvation from sin.

If you're a Christian, you already have the greatest gift in the world: you've been saved.

It's a gift that is on your lips and makes you talk.

In the next chapter, we'll think about another objection: "I'm not really a 'speaking' Christian.

4. SAVED BY THE MOUTH

"I'm not really a 'speaking' Christian."

Maybe you think you're not the kind of person to speak the gospel to others because you're not really the kind of Christian who talks about the gospel. You prefer to keep it in your heart.

But salvation isn't just a matter of the heart. It's also, fundamentally, a matter of the mouth:

> But what does it say? "The word is near you, in your mouth and in your heart" (that is, the word of faith that we proclaim); because, if you confess with your mouth that Jesus is Lord and believe in your heart that God raised him from the dead, you will be saved. For with the heart one believes and is justified, and with the mouth one confesses and is saved. (Rom 10:8-10)

In chapter 2, we looked at human speech from the perspective of Romans 1-3. Every time human speech is mentioned in Romans 1-3, it's a disaster. In fact, the biggest disaster happens when people try to preach God's law: preaching the law creates hypocritical preachers and blaspheming hearers. It's not that God's law is bad. God's law is very good, because it reveals God's will and tells people what they should do to please God. But God's law isn't supposed to be preached. Instead, God's law is supposed to shut our mouths and condemn us. Ultimately, then, God's law is designed to testify to the message of salvation in Jesus Christ. Romans 1-3 renders humans speechless.

All the way up to the end of Romans chapter 9, humans remain almost entirely speechless.[5] The most significant thing humans do in Romans 1-9 is not talk, but "believe" in the message about Jesus Christ. But then something remarkable happens. In chapter 10, people start talking again! Romans 10 mentions testimony (v. 2), preaching (vv. 8, 14, 15), confession (vv. 9, 10), calling on God (vv. 12, 13, 14), and evangelism (vv. 15, 16). There is a message (vv. 8,

---

5   The only clear reference to human speech in Romans 4-9 (apart from Paul's own words) is Romans 8:15; and even here, the emphasis is on the *Spirit* who enables us to cry "Abba! Father!"

17, 18), spoken by believers and preachers; God's gospel-revelation becomes a report (vv. 16, 17) that is heard (vv. 14, 18). Paul also thinks that the mouth is very important; he puts it parallel with the heart as an instrument of salvation (vv. 8, 9, 10, 18). Clearly, speech is very important in Romans 10. Why?

Paul wants to make a contrast in Romans 10, and he wants to spell out this contrast in the starkest possible terms. This contrast is between two ways of salvation (vv. 3-13). The first way of salvation involves the *law*. According to this first way, people become righteous by 'doing' and 'working'; i.e. keeping the law. The second way of salvation, by contrast, involves a *message*, a verbal proclamation, which is opposite to the law (even though the law testifies to it). Since this second way of salvation involves a verbal message, people are righteous by 'believing' and 'confessing' the message, not by 'doing' the law. According to Paul, it's this second way of salvation that is the true and right way. That's why speech is so important.

The gospel of Jesus Christ isn't a law that helps us to be righteous before God by doing good works. The gospel is a *message*, a specific message about a specific person. It's a message that Jesus is Lord, that

God has raised him from the dead. It's a message that God's righteousness comes through this specific person, Jesus the risen Lord. If the gospel of Jesus Christ were a law, the appropriate response to it would be to act, to work, to do good things. But since the gospel of Jesus Christ is a message, we should respond to it first and foremost as a message: by having it in our heart (believing it) and on our lips (confessing it).

Gospel speech, therefore, is not an optional extra for Christians. Salvation comes through a spoken message about a specific person. In God's grace, we are saved through having this message in our hearts and in our mouths. In fact, in a very real sense, we *become* Christian by speaking the gospel. That is, we hear the message that Jesus is Lord, and all it entails, we accept that this message is true, and we 'confess' it. At the very least, this means acknowledging it before God himself; admitting through prayer that Jesus is indeed Lord. And it's not a great leap to confess this message—Jesus is Lord—to other people; for example at church, in baptism, in conversations. So actually, a Christian who prefers not to speak the gospel is a contradiction in terms. Gospel speech is, in fact, at the very core of what it means to be a Christian.

In the next chapter, we'll think about another objection: "I can promote the gospel better by my good works."

5. DO YOU FEEL THE NEED FOR SPEECH?

"I can promote the gospel better by my good works."

Maybe you think you're not the kind of person to speak the gospel to others because your particular role in gospel proclamation is to do good works.

Good works, of course, are something that all Christians are called to do. Doing good works is a responsibility, a privilege, a joy, a struggle, and a way of life (e.g. Eph 2:10; Titus 2:14; Heb 10:24). Good works are the fruit of the gospel, they accompany the gospel, and they adorn the gospel. This is true for every individual Christian person and every Christian group. The Bible never phrases the command "love your neighbour" as if it's an optional role for a select group of specially gifted Christians. We all have different means and opportunities to do good works, but we're all supposed to do good works.

Maybe you've discovered that you're much better at doing good works than you are at speaking the gospel. And maybe you've also noticed how doing good works can be a great advertisement for God's power to transform lives and communities. You've seen that when individual Christians or Christian groups devote themselves to performing good works, the world often sits up and takes notice. The world begins to see that it's good to be one of God's people, because God's people are good people.

So why not, you may ask, let other people do the talking? Don't your works contribute something important to the proclamation of the gospel all by themselves? People can learn by your good works that God's people are good people; and then somebody else can come along later and fill in the key detail: it's all because of Jesus. And then they'll want to be part of God's people too.

But that is the precise problem. Good works without gospel speech do indeed send a message to the world, all by themselves. They tell the world that God's people are good people. Unfortunately, however, that particular message is the precise opposite of the gospel.

In the previous chapter, we looked at the first half of Romans 10. We saw that there's a huge difference between salvation by works of law and salvation by the gospel of Jesus Christ. We're not saved by 'doing' the works of the law. Instead, we're saved by believing and speaking: *believing* in a specific person, Jesus, and *confessing* that he is the Lord, and *calling on* his name (Rom 10:9, 13). This is why gospel speech is at the core of what it means to be a Christian.

But, of course, this isn't just true for you and me. It's true for everyone. Paul is emphatic about this:

> For the Scripture says, "Everyone who believes in him will not be put to shame". (Rom 10:11)

> For "everyone who calls on the name of the Lord will be saved". (Rom 10:13)

And this means that everyone needs to hear, explicitly, the name of the Lord:

> How then will they call on him in whom they have not believed? And how are they to believe in him of whom they have never heard? And how are

they to hear without someone preaching? And how are they to preach unless they are sent? As it is written, "How beautiful are the feet of those who preach the good news!" (Rom 10:14-15)

So faith comes from hearing, and hearing through the word of Christ. (Rom 10:17)

I'm convinced that Paul is talking here about his own Gentile mission.[6] Paul is a preacher (see Rom 10:8) and a 'sent one' (this is what the word 'apostle' means—see Romans 1:1, 5; 11:13)—that's why he talks about the need for preachers who are sent.

Paul's gospel shapes Paul's mission. Since people are saved by responding to a message, they need to *hear* this message. Paul had been sent to preach this very message. That was his mission. Other people in Paul's day believed that their mission was to promote

---

6 If you need to be convinced further about the fact that Romans 10:14-18 is all about the Gentile mission, check out the arguments in NT Wright, 'The Letter to the Romans' in *The New Interpreter's Bible: A Commentary in Twelve Volumes*, NIB, ed. Leander E Keck, 12 vols, vol. 10, Abingdon, Nashville, 2002, p. 667; and Francis Watson, *Paul, Judaism and the Gentiles: Beyond the New Perspective*, rev. and exp. edn, Eerdmans, Grand Rapids, 2007, p. 331. See also John Calvin, *Commentaries on the Epistle of Paul the Apostle to the Romans*, trans. John Owen, Calvin Translation Society, Edinburgh, c. 1847, pp. 396, 404.

God's law (Rom 2:17-24, 10:2-5). Since works are at the core of God's law, doing good works was at the heart of promoting the law. Paul did, of course, believe that doing good works was incredibly important, for a wide variety of reasons (e.g. Romans 12-13). But doing good works wasn't his *mission*. Paul's mission was to promote the gospel, not the law. That meant that speech, not works, was the essential, non-negotiable factor at the heart of gospel proclamation.

It's true that Paul's speaking role was special. Not everybody is Paul. Not everybody is an apostle. Not everybody is *sent* to preach, either. Different people speak the gospel in different ways (more of that later). On the other hand, the basic logic of Romans 10 is something we all need to hear, again and again. People aren't saved by doing good works. People aren't saved by seeing good works, either. People are saved by hearing and speaking a message: "Jesus is Lord". If people were saved by doing good works, then your good works would be an excellent way to directly illustrate and promote what salvation is all about. But because people are saved by hearing and speaking a message, then the only way to proclaim what salvation is all about is by speaking the message.

Do you, like me, believe that good works are not an optional extra for our Christian lives? Do you, like me, believe that every individual Christian should do acts of loving service? Then do them. You don't have to justify your loving actions by using the words 'gospel proclamation' or 'mission'. Just love people, deeply and sacrificially.

But do you also, like me, feel the need for speech? Do you believe that you have been saved not by doing good works, but by hearing and speaking a message: "Jesus is Lord"? Do you believe that others are also saved by hearing and speaking that message? Then keep going the way you started. Keep saying "Jesus is Lord" to yourself and to others.

Do good. But don't stop speaking the gospel.

In the next chapter, we'll think about another objection: "I'm not the mouth in Christ's body."

6. SPEECH IS IN YOUR DNA

"I'm not the mouth in Christ's body."

Paul talks about the church as Christ's body. The body is made up of many members (e.g. 1 Cor 12:12). All of these members are equally important, but they're not all the same. Some people are feet, others are ears, others are eyes, noses, or hands (1 Cor 12:15-26). We all do different things, but we all belong to each other. "So," you might say, "I'm not a mouth. Speaking is not my thing. I have other, equally important, roles in Christ's body." That is, maybe you think you're not the kind of person to speak the gospel to others because you're not that kind of body part.

But there's a problem with this line of reasoning. When Paul talks about the church as Christ's body, he never limits gospel speech to individual body parts.

In fact, Paul makes it crystal clear that gospel speech is something that infuses the whole body.

Let's look at how Paul begins his discussion of the body:

> You know that when you were pagans you were led astray to mute idols, however you were led. Therefore I want you to understand that no one speaking in the Spirit of God ever says "Jesus is accursed!" and no-one can say "Jesus is Lord" except in the Holy Spirit. (1 Cor 12:2-3)

What is the key thing that Paul says about the work of God in individual Christians? God's Spirit creates gospel speech! The Spirit of God is the Spirit who makes us say, "Jesus is Lord". That phrase, "Jesus is Lord", is the heart of the message of salvation. It's exactly the same phrase Paul used in Romans 10:9.[7] A Christian is, in essence, somebody who speaks the right way. By contrast, the definition of idolatry is worshipping things that don't speak (1 Cor 12:2).

So when Paul talks about the church as the body of Christ, he *begins* with gospel speech. The body is a great illustration of unity in diversity. But

---

7   See chapter 4, 'Saved by the mouth'.

it's important to understand what belongs on the 'unity' side of this metaphor, and what belongs on the 'diversity' side. Gospel speech isn't just one of the body parts. At its core, gospel speech is part of the 'unity' side. Gospel speech is fundamental to the body.

When it comes to the body, you have to think about gospel speech in the same way you think about love. 'Love' isn't an optional extra for Christians. Love is a non-negotiable for everyone in the body (check out 1 Corinthians 13). Of course, we'll all love each other in different ways, according to different needs and different circumstances. But it would be crazy, wouldn't it, to divide up Christ's body and assume you can identify people who have the job of being 'loving' and other people who don't have the job of loving others. Love is something for everyone. The same is true of gospel speech. Different people will speak the gospel in different ways. But gospel speech is a non-negotiable factor for each individual in the body. There's no such thing as 'speaking' and 'non-speaking' parts in Christ's body. That's why Paul goes on in 1 Corinthians 14 to urge all the Corinthians to work hard at the right kind of speech: speech that builds the body in love.

You find the same pattern in Ephesians 4:11-16, which is another key passage about the church as the body of Christ. Paul begins by acknowledging that there are some people who have special speaking roles (Eph 4:11):

> And he gave the apostles, the prophets, the evangelists, the shepherds and teachers... (Eph 4:11)

But speech is not limited to these special speakers. The purpose of these special speakers is to help the whole body to speak the truth. Whole-body gospel speech is the ultimate vision for the church:

> Rather, speaking the truth in love, we are to grow up in every way into him who is the head, into Christ, from whom the whole body, joined and held together by every joint with which it is equipped, when each part is working properly, makes the body grow so that it builds itself up in love. (Eph 4:15-16)

The 'truth' that builds the body is the gospel of Jesus Christ, which is a spoken message (cf. Eph 1:13, 4:21). When it comes to the body of Christ, gospel speech isn't restricted to any one body part. Gospel speech and love are the basis and the means by which all the other parts of the body grow.

Gospel speech (along with love) isn't just one of the body parts. It's really more like DNA. DNA is the basic molecular code that sits in the nucleus of every individual cell in our bodies. Different cells grow in different ways and make up different body parts. But they are united by the same basic code: the DNA. In the same way, gospel speech is part of the basic reality that informs all of our other actions and relationships in Christ's body. Different members of Christ's body will speak (and live out) the gospel in different ways. But gospel speech permeates everything.

But hang on, you might say, this whole "speaking the truth in love" thing is about how I relate to insiders, isn't it? What does it have to do with speaking to outsiders? In the next chapter, we'll look at that very issue. Is there a difference between speaking the gospel to insiders and speaking the gospel to outsiders?

7. INSIDERS AND OUTSIDERS

"I'm more comfortable speaking the gospel to insiders rather than outsiders."

Maybe you think you're not the kind of person to speak the gospel to outsiders because you're more comfortable speaking to insiders. But gospel speech doesn't work that way. The gospel, by its very nature, breaks through distinctions between 'insiders' and 'outsiders'. And so does gospel speech.

This is a staggering truth. Even the great apostle Peter had problems grasping its implications. Peter, like Paul, was Jewish, which means he had the great privilege of growing up knowing God's law. The law revealed God's will to his people. The job of law-keepers was to honour God by obeying him and to remain pure by avoiding evil influences. So they did what was right and avoided the 'sinners' all around them, who threatened to corrupt them and move them away from pure devotion to God. Classic law-keepers, therefore, made a big deal out of the distinction between 'insiders' (law-keepers) and 'outsiders' (sinners). Peter had previously come to know and trust Jesus, and had stopped insisting on this distinction. But later, he reverted to his former way of life because he was afraid of other classic law-keepers:

> For before certain men came from James, he [Peter] was eating with the Gentiles; but when they came he drew back and separated himself, fearing the circumcision party. (Gal 2:12)

The problem with Peter's behaviour wasn't simply that it was cowardly, exclusivist, elitist, racist, or anything-else-ist. The problem went much deeper. When Peter separated from outsiders so publicly, he undermined the truth of the gospel itself (Gal 2:14). The gospel declares that everybody, whether insider or outsider, has the same problem and needs exactly the same solution. We're all sinners, and we all need to be justified by God through trusting in Jesus. Whether we're an insider or an outsider, whatever our history or status or reputation, makes no difference. When the gospel is spoken and believed, law-keepers are shown to be sinners, and 'sinners' are given access to salvation through trusting Christ Jesus (Gal 2:15-17). At its core, the gospel says the same thing to the people sitting in your church as it does to the people walking down your street.

Of course, there will be differences about the *way* we speak the gospel to different people. When we speak the gospel to outsiders, it's usually harder. It takes longer to speak with outsiders because they don't have our shared experiences, which make communication easy and efficient. We have to try to avoid or explain jargon that only makes sense to insiders; we need to be more aware of the possibility of being misunderstood. More significantly, the risks of rejection are much higher when we speak the gospel to outsiders. They don't necessarily agree with us, and they might be very upset. Speaking the gospel to outsiders isn't necessarily going to be comfortable. But love drives us to speak to them, and our comfort isn't a factor according to the Bible. In fact, the places where the Bible talks most explicitly about speaking up for Jesus are places where opposition is clearly in view (e.g. Phil 1:27-30; Col 4:2-6; 1 Pet 3:14-16). Speaking the gospel to outsiders is more important than our individual comfort levels.

The gospel is the great equalizer; it breaks down distinctions between insiders and outsiders. The gospel message is ultimately the same for everybody. If you can speak the gospel to insiders, you can speak the gospel to outsiders too. And, if you love them, you will.

In the next chapter, we'll think about a final objection: "I can't do what they're doing."

8. LEARNING HOW TO TALK

"I can't do what they're doing."

Maybe you're convinced that gospel speech is at the very core of what it means to be a Christian. Maybe you're convinced that the world needs to hear the gospel. But you look around and you see real live gospel speakers. You watch them closely and listen to the way they talk. Then you look at yourself, your own speaking abilities, your own background, your own life situation. And you realize, with a mixture of bewilderment, disappointment, and maybe even a twinge of jealousy, that you're not like those gospel speakers. You don't have their gift. How could you ever do evangelism like they do it?

Oops, there's that word again: 'evangelism'—the word I said was going to avoid. Now that I've said it again, I might as well ask you what images it conjures up in your head. Who do you think of as 'evangelists':

- The crazy street preacher on a soap box?
- The smart guy who's memorized a gospel outline and knows how to use it in a variety of contexts, even backwards if required?
- The stadium speaker who preaches his heart out and gets thousands coming forward to know more?
- The Christian supermum who not only looks after her husband and five kids but also writes evangelistic books, speaks at evangelistic coffee and chocolate nights and updates her trendy yet tastefully decorated blog twice a day?
- The person who effortlessly strikes up conversations in supermarkets, bus queues and taxis, and invariably turns them into conversations that are all about Jesus *but at the same time aren't weird*? (How do they do it?)
- The serial inviter who invites fifteen friends to every evangelistic coffee and chocolate night, and all of the friends come?
- The 'full-time' ministers?

Most of what we learn in life comes from following the example of others. Children copy their parents; younger kids look up to older kids; students are inspired by passionate teachers. It's the same with speaking the gospel. In this area, like many areas in life, role models are a gift from God (check out 1 Cor 11:1; Phil 3:17; 1 Thess 1:6; Heb 13:7). We need real-life flesh-and-blood examples of gospel speech in operation. But if you focus too closely on these role models, you end up with a problem. You think that you have to speak the gospel exactly like they do. And you're afraid that if you can't speak the gospel like they speak the gospel, you're not a gospel speaker at all. Sometimes, specially gifted gospel speakers can make the problem worse. They can be so passionately committed to their own way of doing evangelism that they end up faithfully reproducing their own methods, instead of faithfully reproducing the gospel itself.

Given this problem, what should you do?

Firstly, keep remembering to rejoice in specially gifted gospel speakers. They are members of Christ's body, and therefore they are united with us in faith and love. Don't envy them. Acknowledge that they are God's gifts to his people. Listen to them, encourage them, love them and support them. Express your fellowship in the gospel with them, both prayerfully and, if they need it, financially, so that the gospel can go forward. If you think other people in the world need them, send them out!

Secondly, treat them as role models. Learn to imitate specially gifted gospel speakers wherever you can. They're there to enable the whole body to grow and change and speak the gospel more and more (Eph 4:11-16). Remember that no matter which 'body part' you may be now, your role isn't fixed for life. Just because you can't do something today doesn't mean you'll never be able to. As I think back over the almost 30 years I've been a Christian, I realize how grateful I am to various gospel-speaking role models who pushed me beyond my comfort zone. Sometimes they did it simply by their own example; sometimes they explicitly urged me to try new things. Either way, they spurred me on to speak the gospel in ways that were unfamiliar, scary, and highly worthwhile. Growth can be painful. But at least when you're growing, you know you're alive.

Thirdly, and most importantly, keep focusing on and delighting in the gospel of Jesus Christ himself, not in particular gospel speakers. Keep growing in your knowledge and love of the gospel. Don't ever say that you've got the gospel sorted out; never claim that you understand everything there is to know about the gospel. You can never master God's word. God is too powerful for that. Through his word and Spirit, God judges you, transforms you, changes you, moulds you into his child, and puts his words in your heart and on your lips. And he keeps doing it, every day. It's living and active. That's why it is so important to keep soaking yourself in the Bible. "Jesus is Lord" is the gospel. But it's a very short sentence. The Bible is the extended version. The Bible will give you the breadth and depth of insight you need to understand how you might speak the gospel into your own particular situation.

Finally, learn to understand yourself in the light of the gospel. God speaks to each one of us where we're at. We have different life circumstances, different webs of relationships, different personalities, different skills, different knowledge, different motivations. We love different things and we know different people. So everybody speaks the gospel differently. I've enjoyed reading Tony Payne and Colin Marshall's book, *The Trellis and the Vine*, because it makes this precise point. All Christians are supposed to be speaking Christians. But there are an infinite number of different ways for Christians to speak (check out, for example, the various ideas on pages

54-55 of that book).

How many different ways can you think of for Christians to speak the gospel? Here are just a few ways in which I've been personally encouraged by great gospel speakers.

- There's a bloke I know on disability benefits who used to live in a share home. His housemates knew he was a Christian and gave him flak for it. He wrote letters to me regularly about his struggles and failures and joys in knowing and living for Jesus, and told me he was praying for me.

- Jean, once a month, gets together with a group of other school mums to pray for families at the school. Together, they use the opportunities that God gives them to build relationships that will lead to meaningful conversations about Jesus.

- There's a retired gentleman I know who sings songs in church very loudly and completely out of tune, with obvious joy in his heart. It's fantastic.

- There's a student I know who gets barraged by her coursemates with questions and objections to the gospel. She tells them how Jesus makes a difference in her own life, answers their questions when she can, tries to find out more so she can be better equipped, and invites her coursemates and Christian friends to share meals together and talk further about the issues.

- There's a kid I know who was asked to do a school project on rainbows, and wrote about God's promise to Noah not to flood the world again.

"Are all Christians commanded to evangelize?" I hope I've convinced you by now on how many levels that question is wrong. The real question is this: what is the gospel (i.e. the good news that transforms my heart and my speech)? And the second question is: how can I love the people around me and speak it in my particular circumstances?

These are questions that I hope you'll spend a lifetime answering.

APPENDIX: QUESTIONS FOR DISCUSSION OR PERSONAL REFLECTION

DIFFERENT KINDS OF GOSPEL SPEECH

Step 1: Brainstorm

Write down all the different kinds of gospel speech you can. Think of concrete examples of gospel speech that you've seen in action, but also think creatively about possibilities you might not have seen.

Step 2: Eliminate

Should any of the things you listed during the brainstorm be eliminated—either because they're just ridiculous (even if they were fun to raise during the brainstorm), or because they aren't really examples of gospel speech at all?

Step 3: Apply

Think about yourself—your experiences, gifts, preferences. Now categorize the different kinds of gospel speech you wrote down into the following three types (over the page). The answers will be different for each person!

For each of the three different kinds of gospel speech you list, write down an example.

Then, for each example, answer the questions on page 62. Pray that God will help you to keep speaking the truth in love to many around you.

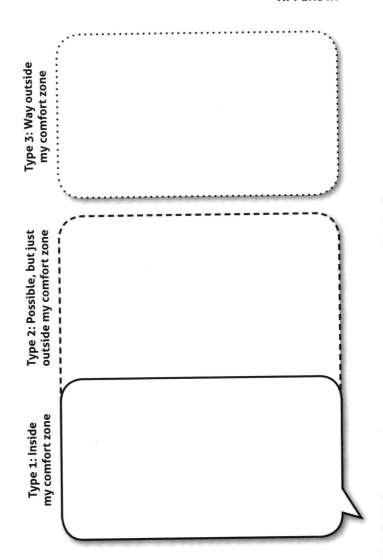

Type 3: Way outside
my comfort zone

Type 2: Possible, but just
outside my comfort zone

Type 1: Inside
my comfort zone

GOSPEL SPEECH

Type 3: Way outside my comfort zone

Kind of gospel speech:

How can I support and encourage other people to speak the gospel in this way? For example, can I pray, or provide practical help, or financial support?

Type 2: Possible, but just outside my comfort zone

Kind of gospel speech:

What practical steps can I take to make sure I speak the gospel in this way more and more?

How can I act as a role model to others in this area? For example, can I encourage or help other people to speak the gospel in this way?

Type 1: Inside my comfort zone

Kind of gospel speech:

What practical steps can I take to move beyond my comfort zone and try to engage in this kind of gospel speech more?

What role models can I learn from as I'm doing this?

Matthias Media is an evangelical publishing ministry that seeks to persuade all Christians of the truth of God's purposes in Jesus Christ as revealed in the Bible, and equip them with high-quality resources, so that by the work of the Holy Spirit they will:

- abandon their lives to the honour and service of Christ in daily holiness and decision-making
- pray constantly in Christ's name for the fruitfulness and growth of his gospel
- speak the Bible's life-changing word whenever and however they can—in the home, in the world and in the fellowship of his people.

Our resources range from Bible studies and books through to training courses, audio sermons and children's Sunday School material. To find out more, and to access samples and free downloads, visit our website:

www.matthiasmedia.com

How to buy our resources

1. Direct from us over the internet:
   – in the US: www.matthiasmedia.com
   – in Australia: www.matthiasmedia.com.au

2. Direct from us by phone: please visit our website for current phone contact information.

> Register at our website for our **free** regular email update to receive information about the latest new resources, **exclusive special offers**, and free articles to help you grow in your Christian life and ministry.

3. Through a range of outlets in various parts of the world. Visit **www.matthiasmedia.com/contact** for details about recommended retailers in your part of the world, including www.thegoodbook.co.uk in the United Kingdom.

4. Trade enquiries can be addressed to:
   – in the US and Canada: sales@matthiasmedia.com
   – in Australia and the rest of the world: sales@matthiasmedia.com.au

5. Visit **GoThereFor.com** for subscription-based access to a great-value range of digital resources.

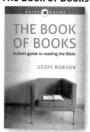
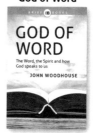

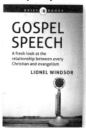
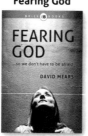
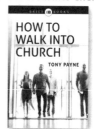